Pro Stock Cars

By Muriel L. Dubois

Consultant:
The International
Motorsports Hall of Fame

CAPSTONE
HIGH-INTEREST
BOOKS

an imprint of Capstone Press
Mankato, Minnesota

Capstone High-Interest Books are published by Capstone Press
151 Good Counsel Drive, P.O. Box 669, Mankato, Minnesota 56002
http://www.capstone-press.com

Library of Congress Cataloging-in-Publication Data
Dubois, Muriel L.
   Pro stock cars/by Muriel L. Dubois.
   p. cm.—(Wild rides!)
   Includes bibliographical references and index.
   ISBN 0-7368-0931-7
   1. Stock cars (Automobiles)—Juvenile literature. 2. Stock car
racing—Juvenile literature. [1. Stock cars (Automobiles) 2. Stock car racing.]
I. Title. II. Series.
TL236.28 .D83 2002
629.228—dc21   2001000214

Summary: Discusses these race cars, their history, parts, and the NASCAR races
that make them famous.

Editorial Credits
Matt Doeden, editor; Karen Risch, product planning editor; Kia Bielke,
   cover designer and illustrator; Katy Kudela, photo researcher

Photo Credits
Active Images, Inc./Greg Crisp, 28
ALLSPORT PHOTOGRAPHY, cover, 4 (bottom), 6–7, 10 (bottom), 26
Isaac Hernandez/Mercury Press, 4 (top), 16
Peter Gridley/FPG International LLC, 12
SportsChrome-USA/Brian Spurlock, 8, 22 (top); Greg Crisp, 10 (top), 14, 19,
20, 22 (bottom), 25

1 2 3 4 5 6 07 06 05 04 03 02

Table of Contents

Learn about:

- Stock cars in action

- Stock car models

- Stock car teams

Pro Stock Cars

Forty-three drivers slowly circle the racetrack at the Daytona International Speedway in Daytona Beach, Florida. The drivers come around the track's fourth turn and wait for the starting signal.

The flagman waves the green flag to begin the race. The drivers reach speeds of more than 200 miles (322 kilometers) per hour. They stay tightly together at first. But two cars slowly pull ahead of the rest.

The lead car slowly increases its lead over the second-place car. The drivers then have to go into the pits for new tires and more fuel. Each driver's pit crew works to get the car back onto the racetrack quickly. But the lead car's pit crew has trouble changing a tire. The car stays in the pits too long. The car loses its place at the front of the pack.

The race has a new leader when the cars come out of the pits. But the other drivers do not give up. The race is 500 miles (805 kilometers) long. They have plenty of time to catch the leader.

About Stock Cars

Pro stock car racing is one of the most popular sports in North America. Drivers race around oval tracks at speeds of more than 200 miles (322 kilometers) per hour.

Stock cars are based on standard street cars. These cars have a similar body shape. But stock cars are built to be far more powerful.

Their engines can accelerate quickly to reach high speeds.

All stock cars are based on one of four types of street cars. They are the Chevrolet Monte Carlo, the Ford Taurus, the Pontiac Grand Prix, and the Dodge Intrepid. These cars are about equal in racing performance. This equality keeps the races fair.

Most professional stock cars are colorful. They have many advertisements and logos painted on them. A logo is a symbol of a company. For example, a stock car may have the logo of an oil company on its hood. The oil company pays the stock car's owner to place the logo there.

Stock cars have a similar body shape to standard cars.

A pit crew keeps a stock car in top working order during a race.

Race Teams

The driver is not the only member of a stock car team. The pit crew also is important to the car's performance. Pit crews include mechanics who work on the car before, during, and after a race. Pit crew members select the best tires for a race. They make sure the engine is in top working order. Pit crews must make quick adjustments during a race. A car will lose its place on the track if pit crews work slowly.

Stock car teams also include owners and sponsors. Owners select drivers and pit crews for their cars. Sponsors provide most of the money for pro stock car teams. This money allows the teams to buy the expensive parts needed to keep the cars running. Sponsors also have logos on the cars. A team's main sponsor usually has a logo on the car's hood.

Most professional stock car teams take part in NASCAR events. NASCAR stands for the National Association of Stock Car Automobile Racing. Professional drivers and pit crew members earn their living by taking part in these NASCAR events.

CHAPTER **2**

Early Models of Pro Stock Cars

Car racing became popular during the 1930s. People gathered at places such as Daytona Beach, Florida. They raced their cars on the sand. At first, the races were not organized. But soon, people set up tracks on the beach. They added driving rules. Fans sometimes bet money on which driver would win each race. The races grew more popular every year.

Early race cars were modified street cars.

NASCAR is Born

A driver and mechanic named Bill France became interested in the Daytona Beach races. In 1938, France organized his own race. He quickly learned that he could make money by setting up races. France then became a full-time race organizer.

Early race cars were not specially built. They were just street cars. But many of the drivers modified their cars. They made small changes to the engine or body design to improve the car's performance.

In 1947, France held a meeting with drivers, mechanics, and race sponsors. France believed that his races needed more formal rules. He hoped these rules would increase the popularity of the sport. Some of the group members wrote a set of stock car racing rules. The group began using the name NASCAR.

Richard Petty was one of the first NASCAR stars.

Stock Car Changes

NASCAR helped make stock car racing a popular sport. Car manufacturers saw that people would notice which types of cars won the races. These manufacturers began to build cars just for stock car racing. They hoped that these cars would help increase sales of their street cars.

Manufacturers began to change stock cars. They made the engines more powerful and efficient. They also added safety features to the cars. These features included roll cages. These systems of metal tubes strengthened the car's body. The roll cages provided extra protection to drivers during crashes.

Racing continued to grow in popularity throughout the 1950s and 1960s. France helped build paved tracks such as the Daytona International Speedway. Drivers such as Richard Petty and David Pearson became popular with fans. NASCAR races began to appear on TV. Stock car racing had quickly become one of the most popular sports in North America.

Learn about:

■ **The chassis**

■ **Wheels and suspension systems**

■ **Racing features**

Designing a Pro Stock Car

Pro stock car drivers and mechanics work together to build the fastest cars. Some team members are responsible for a car's engine. Others are designers who work on a car's body. They study different body shapes to reduce air resistance. Air-resistant body shapes reduce the force of air that slows down a moving object.

Body Design

Teams start with factory parts. The hood, roof, front grill, and bumpers come from the factory. They are the same parts used in street cars. Every other part of a stock car is specially made for racing.

The main part of a stock car's body is the chassis. This strong metal frame supports the body of the car. All the other parts connect to the chassis.

The wheels connect to the chassis on strong axles. Wide rubber tires fit over the wheels. Stock car tires are made of smooth, sticky rubber. The tires are able to grip paved track surfaces at high speeds.

Suspension systems help absorb many of the bumps on a racetrack. Shock absorbers are connected to each of the wheels. The shock absorbers include springs. The springs allow the tires to travel smoothly over small bumps.

Engine Design

Stock cars have engines similar to those found in street cars. But stock car engines are more powerful. They also burn fuel more quickly. A stock car may travel only about 3 miles (4.8 kilometers) for each gallon of fuel it burns. Most street cars travel at least 20 miles (32 kilometers) on each gallon of fuel.

Stock car engines have eight cylinders. Fuel burns inside these pipe-shaped chambers. The fuel provides the energy to power the car. People measure engine power in horsepower. Engines in street cars produce about 150 horsepower. Stock car engines may produce 750 horsepower or more.

Stock car engines are built to produce a great deal of power.

Air dams prevent air from flowing under a stock car.

Other Features

Stock cars do not have some of the features that street cars have. For example, stock cars do not have doors. Drivers must climb in and out of the cars through the windows. Stock cars also have only one seat.

Stock cars include some parts most street cars do not have. Teams add a spoiler to the back of the car. A spoiler looks like an airplane wing. It helps keep the car on the track. Teams also add an air dam to the front of the car. This part sits low to the ground. It prevents air from flowing under the car. At high speeds, air could lift the car and make it unstable.

The inside of a stock car also is different from the inside of a street car. Every piece of unnecessary equipment is removed from stock cars to reduce weight. Stock cars do not have speedometers to tell drivers how fast they are going. But stock cars do have other gauges inside. These instruments help the driver know the condition of the engine. The driver can make a pit stop if the engine is not running properly.

Learn about:

- **Types of tracks**

- **Winston Cup racing**

- **Qualifying**

CHAPTER **4**

Pro Stock Cars in Competition

Today, stock car racing is one of the most popular sports in North America. Many drivers race stock cars for a living. Some earn millions of dollars each year. This money comes from sponsorships, race winnings, and endorsements. Racers endorse products by appearing in advertisements.

Tracks

Stock car races take place on tracks in many North American cities. Most stock car tracks are large ovals. They include two long straightaways. Cars can reach the highest speeds on these long, straight sections. The two straightaways are connected by two curved sections.

Not all stock car tracks are ovals. Some are tri-oval tracks. These tracks do not have two equal straightaways. One side of the track curves outward to form a shape like a large letter D. Other tracks are road-course tracks. These tracks have many turns and very short straightaways.

Stock cars race on tracks of different lengths. Short tracks are less than 1 mile (1.6 kilometers) long. Intermediate tracks are between 1 and 2 miles (1.6 and 3.2 kilometers) long. Superspeedways are longer than 2 miles.

NASCAR Circuits

NASCAR holds races in circuits. On circuits, race teams take part in a series of races. They earn points for each race depending on their finish. The team with the most points after all of the races wins the circuit championship.

The Winston Cup Series is the most popular NASCAR circuit. Most Winston Cup races are between 400 and 600 miles (644 and 966 kilometers) long. The Winston Cup Series includes famous races such as the Daytona 500.

NASCAR also holds the Busch Grand National Series. This circuit is similar to the

Winston Cup Series. But the races in this circuit are shorter. Most Busch Grand National Series races are between 200 and 300 miles (322 and 483 kilometers) long.

Most NASCAR races take place on oval tracks such as the Martinsville Speedway in Virginia.

The Race

Race teams must qualify for a race before taking part. Each driver goes onto the track alone to qualify. The driver goes as fast as possible

A flagman waves a green flag to begin a race.

around the track. Officials record the fastest lap. The driver with the fastest lap begins the race in first place, or the pole position. The rest of the racers start behind the pole position according to their times.

Drivers must watch the flagman. This race official waves colored flags during the race. The flagman waves a green flag to begin the race. A yellow flag warns drivers of dangers such as a crash on the track. The flagman waves a white flag when one lap remains in the race. A checkered flag tells drivers that the final lap has ended.

The winner of a stock car race sometimes takes a victory lap. The racer drives slowly around the track and waves to the fans. The driver then goes into the victory lane. Race officials give the driver a trophy in the victory lane. The winning driver and team celebrate together. But their celebration does not last long. They know that they must begin preparing for the next race.

Jeff Gordon

Jeff Gordon is one of the most popular drivers on NASCAR's Winston Cup circuit. Gordon was born August 4, 1971, in Vallejo, California. At age 5, he began racing small vehicles called quarter midgets. He continued racing throughout his childhood.

Gordon began racing stock cars in 1991. He started on NASCAR's Busch Grand National Series. In 1992, he moved to NASCAR's Winston Cup Series. In 1993, Gordon was named NASCAR's rookie of the year. This award goes to Winston Cup's best first-year driver.

Gordon quickly became one of the best stock car drivers in the world. He won the Winston Cup Championship in 1995, 1997, and 1998. In 1998, he won four races in a row. Only racing greats Richard Petty and Bobby Allison had accomplished that feat.

Words to Know

accelerate (ak-SEL-uh-rate)—to gain speed

axle (AK-suhl)—a rod in the center of a wheel around which the wheel turns

chassis (CHASS-ee)—the frame on which the body of a vehicle is built

cylinder (SIL-uhn-dur)—a hollow chamber inside an engine in which fuel is burned to create power

flagman (FLAG-man)—a race official who uses colored flags to give drivers information about racing conditions

modify (MOD-uh-fye)—to change; racing teams modify a car or engine in order to make it faster or more powerful

spoiler (SPOY-luhr)—a wing-like device attached to the back of a stock car; spoilers help keep cars stable on the track.

suspension system (suh-SPEN-shuhn SISS-tuhm)—the system of springs and shock absorbers that absorbs up-and-down movement from the axles

To Learn More

Center, Bill, and Bob Moore. *NASCAR 50 Greatest Drivers.* New York: HarperHorizon, 1998.

Mara, W. P. *Pro Stock Car Racing.* MotorSports. Mankato, Minn.: Capstone Books, 1999.

McGuire, Ann. *The History of NASCAR.* Race Car Legends. Philadelphia: Chelsea House, 2000.

Useful Addresses

Daytona International Speedway Visitors Center
1801 West International Speedway Boulevard
Daytona Beach, FL 32114-1243

International Motorsports Hall of Fame
P.O. Box 1018
Talladega, AL 35161

Motorsports Hall of Fame of America
43700 Expo Center Drive
Novi, MI 48376

Internet Sites

International Motorsports Hall of Fame
http://www.motorsportshalloffame.com

NASCAR.com
http://www.NASCAR.com

Talladega Superspeedway
http://www.talladegasuperspeedway.com

Index